EAT, PRAY, LOVE
One Woman's Search for Everything

There comes a time in everybody's life when the big questions hit you. Who am I? What's it all about? What have I done with my life so far? Where am I going? What do I want? Should I change my house . . . change my job, my marriage, my life?

At the age of thirty-one Elizabeth Gilbert realizes that she doesn't want babies, doesn't want to be married anymore, and doesn't know what she wants from life. A difficult divorce and a wild affair with a new lover bring heartbreak, depression, and despair. She asks an old Balinese medicine man for advice. How can she find balance in her life? 'You must have your feet strongly on the ground,' he tells her. 'But you must not look at the world through your head. You must look through your heart.'

So she begins her search. In Italy she explores pleasure through her love of the Italian language and Italian food. In India she finds a path to devotion through meditation and prayer in an Ashram. And in Indonesia she finds something wonderful, something she never expected to find again . . .

OXFORD BOOKWORMS LIBRARY
True Stories

Eat, Pray, Love
One Woman's Search for Everything

Stage 4 (1400 headwords)

Series Editor: Jennifer Bassett
Founder Editor: Tricia Hedge
Activities Editors: Jennifer Bassett and Christine Lindop

AUTHOR'S NOTE

I offer thanks to all my teachers, who have appeared before me this year in so many different ways. But most of all I thank my Guru, who so generously allowed me to study at her Ashram while I was in India. I would like to explain that I write about my own experiences in India and give my own opinions and beliefs. I do not write as a student of religion or as somebody who speaks for an organization. This is why I do not use my Guru's name throughout this book – because I cannot speak for her. Her teachings speak best for themselves. And in order to save the Ashram from unwanted publicity, I give neither its name nor its address.

Elizabeth Gilbert

ELIZABETH GILBERT

Eat, Pray, Love

One Woman's Search for Everything

Retold by
Rachel Bladon

Illustrated by
Kali Ciesemier

OXFORD UNIVERSITY PRESS

OXFORD

UNIVERSITY PRESS

Great Clarendon Street, Oxford, OX2 6DP, United Kingdom

Oxford University Press is a department of the University of Oxford.
It furthers the University's objective of excellence in research, scholarship,
and education by publishing worldwide. Oxford is a registered trade
mark of Oxford University Press in the UK and in certain other countries

This simplified edition © Oxford University Press 2014

The moral rights of the author have been asserted

First published in Oxford Bookworms 2014

19

Original edition copyright © Elizabeth Gilbert 2006

First published in Great Britain by Bloomsbury Publishing Plc 2006

The right of Elizabeth Gilbert to be identified as author of this work has been asserted.

ISBN: 978 0 19 478616 4

A complete recording of this Bookworms edition of
Eat, Pray, Love is available in an audio pack. ISBN: 978 0 19 478606 5

Printed in China

Word count (main text): 18,805

For more information on the Oxford Bookworms Library,
visit www.oup.com/elt/gradedreaders

ACKNOWLEDGEMENTS
Illustrated by: Kali Ciesemier/The Loud Cloud

CONTENTS

PEOPLE IN THIS STORY

Elizabeth Gilbert (Liz)

AMERICA
Liz's ex-husband
David, *Liz's lover*
Susan, *Liz's best friend*
Nick, *son of Liz's sister*

ITALY
Giovanni, *Liz's Exchange Partner*
Sofie, *a Swedish friend from language classes*
Maria and Giulio, *friends*
Luca Spaghetti, *a friend*
Linda, *a friend from America*
Mario and Simona, *friends of Luca Spaghetti*
Deborah, *a friend from America*

INDIA
Arturo, *a young Mexican man at the Ashram*
Richard from Texas, *a friend at the Ashram*
Delia, *an Australian woman, one of Liz's room-mates*

INDONESIA
Ketut Liyer, *a Balinese medicine man*
Nyomo, *Ketut Liyer's wife*
Mario, *a Balinese man working in the hotel in Ubud*
Wayan Nuriyasih, *a Balinese healer*
Tutti, *Wayan's daughter*
Felipe, *a Brazilian man, Liz's lover*
Yudhi, *a Balinese friend*

The Beginning

It is midnight and foggy, and Giovanni is walking me home to my apartment through the back streets of Rome. We are at my door, and he gives me a warm hug.

'Good night, my dear Liz,' he says.

'*Buona notte, caro mio,*' I reply. Good night, my dear.

I want Giovanni to kiss me, but there are so many reasons why this would be a terrible idea. First, Giovanni is ten years younger than me, and – like most young Italian men – he lives with his mother. This doesn't make him a good partner for me – an American woman writer, aged thirty-four, who has just come through a failed marriage and an endless, heartbreaking divorce, followed by a love affair that also ended in heartbreak. These experiences have left me feeling sad, lonely, and about seven thousand years old. So it wouldn't be right for lovely young Giovanni to have a sorry, broken woman like me. And anyway, I am finally old enough to know what is good for me. I have decided to spend this year without a man in my life. I am not looking for a relationship. I am looking for the kind of healing and peace that can only come from being alone.

Giovanni is my Exchange Partner. This means we meet a few evenings a week here in Rome to speak each other's languages. We speak first in Italian, and he is patient with me; then we speak in English, and I am patient with him. We only talk. Well, we eat and we talk. We have been eating and talking for many weeks now, and tonight has been another lovely evening of pizza and new words.

So why am I in Italy, spending my time with a handsome young Italian man who will not kiss me? My story begins three years earlier, on the bathroom floor of my house in New York. It was a cold November, around three o'clock in the morning. My husband was sleeping in our bed, and I was hiding in the bathroom and crying, as I had done for about forty-seven nights before.

'I don't want to be married anymore,' a voice inside my head was saying. 'I don't want to live in this big house. I don't want to have a baby.'

My husband and I had been married for six years, and we had built our lives around the idea that we would have children when I was thirty. We thought that by then I would be happy to live in a big busy house full of children, with a garden at the back and supper cooking in the kitchen. But I was shocked to find that, as my twenties came to an end, I didn't want any of those things. I kept waiting to want to have a baby, but it didn't happen.

I told myself that this was normal. All women must feel this way before they have children, I decided. But every night, I just couldn't stop thinking, 'I don't want to be married anymore.' Why was I feeling like this? Hadn't I wanted to buy this nice house, just a year ago? Wasn't I proud of everything we had – this house, the apartment in Manhattan, the friends, and the parties? I had helped to build this life of ours, so why now was it just not right for me? Why did I suddenly feel so tired of everything – tired of working every day, of organizing our home life and our evenings out, of being a wife and, in the few free moments I could find, a writer?

My husband and I had been fighting and crying for months, and we were exhausted and sad. I still loved him, and I couldn't imagine life without him. The only thing that felt more impossible than staying with him was leaving him.

But on this cold November night, three years ago, something happened that would change my life forever.

What happened was that I started to pray.

You know – like, to *God*.

In the last three years, I've done a lot of thinking about God, and what I believe is very simple. It's like this: I used to have a great dog. She had about ten different kinds of dog in her, but she seemed to have the best bits of all of them. She was brown. When people asked me, 'What kind of dog is that?' I always answered, 'She's a brown dog.' In the same way, when people ask me 'What kind of God do you believe in?' my answer is easy: 'I believe in a magnificent God.'

But at that time, I didn't know what I believed. I just knew that I was starting to feel dangerously hopeless and desperate, and I knew that at times like these, people often ask God for help.

What I said to God that night, crying my heart out, was something like this: 'Hello, God. How are you? I'm Liz. I'm sorry that I haven't really spoken to you before. I do hope I have been thankful enough for all the many things you have given me.'

This thought made me cry even harder, so it was a while

before I could go on. 'I'm not good at praying, as you know, but please can you help me? I don't know what to do. Please tell me what to do!' The crying went on and on. I was like a woman trying to save her own life.

And then, suddenly, the crying stopped. I looked up, wondering if I would see this Great God who had taken my tears away. Nobody was there. I was alone. But I felt that there was something surrounding me, something I can only describe as a special kind of silence. I have never felt so still and quiet.

Then I heard a voice – just my voice, coming from inside me. But I had never heard my voice sound like this before. It was calm and sensible, and it said, *Go back to bed, Liz.* And I could see at once that this was the only thing I could do. *Go back to bed*, because you can't know the answer at three o'clock in the morning on a Thursday in November. *Go back to bed*, and rest until you do know the answer. *Go back to bed*, and then when the day comes, you will be strong enough. And that was the beginning of a religious conversation that would, in the end, bring me very close to God.

Seven very difficult months later, I did leave my husband. When I finally decided to do that, I thought the worst time was over. That shows how little I knew about divorce.

My husband and I had once known each other better than anyone in the world. Suddenly we could not understand each other. He never believed that I would leave him, and I never thought he would make it so difficult for me to go. I really believed when I left him that we could organize everything in a few hours. I thought we would sell the house and each take half of everything. But my husband did not think this was fair, and we could not agree about our divorce.

And then there was David. All the disasters of those ugly divorce years were made ten times worse by my affair with David – the guy I fell in love with at that time. I jumped out of my marriage and into David's arms, and put every hope I had for happiness and healing into our relationship.

I moved into David's apartment right after I left my husband. He was – is – a beautiful young man. A born New Yorker, an actor and a writer, sure of himself, spiritual, and sexy. The first time my best friend Susan heard me talking about him, she took one look at me and said, 'Oh my God, you are in so much trouble.'

We had such a great time together during those early months. We went on day trips and road trips. We climbed to the top of things, swam to the bottom of other things, talked about the journeys across the world that we would take together. We made plans, promises, and dinner together. The first summer of Liz and David looked like the falling-in-love part of every romantic movie you've ever seen. At this time I was still thinking my divorce would go OK – that my husband and I were just having a break from talking about things over the summer because we both needed to cool down. Then that summer ended.

On September 9, 2001, I met with my husband for the last time. We had dinner in a restaurant, and tried to talk about our separation, but we could only fight. He told me that he hated me and would never speak to me again. Two mornings later I woke up after a bad night's sleep and found that airplanes were crashing into the two tallest buildings of my city. I called my husband because I wanted to know that he was safe. We cried together, but I did not go to him. During that week, when everyone in New York forgot their arguments because of the terrible thing that had happened in our city, I still did not go back to my husband. And so we both knew that our marriage was over.

After that, I really didn't sleep much for the next four months. I thought things had been bad before, but now my life really fell to pieces. Imagine David's surprise to discover that the happiest, most confident woman he'd ever met was actually a dark hole of terrible sadness. I could not stop crying. This is when David started to pull away from me, and that's when I saw the other side of him: the David who was cool, who needed to be alone, who didn't want to be touched. The more he pulled away, the more I needed him. My marriage had failed, terrible things had happened to my city, I was going through the worst ugliness of divorce, and now I was losing David. This was simply too much.

Night-times became terrifying for me. Every night I lay awake, desperate, feeling the most terrible loneliness, and wanting to kill myself. Most mornings, David woke to find me on the floor next to his bed, like a dog.

'What happened now?' he asked, day after day – another man completely exhausted by me.

I think I lost about fourteen kilos during that time.

———

But it wasn't all bad, those few years. A few wonderful things did happen to me in the shadow of all that sadness.

First, I finally started learning Italian. Also, I found my Indian Guru. And I was asked by an old medicine man to come and live with him in Indonesia.

Things started to get better when, in early 2002, I moved into an apartment on my own, for the first time in my life. I painted the walls in the warmest colors I could find, and bought myself flowers every week.

David and I had ended our affair. Or had we? We separated and got back together so many times over those months. Every time I separated from David, I grew stronger and more confident again, and he fell in love with me once more. So then we tried again – because how could two people who were so in love not be happy together? But then David pulled away from me again and I held on to him. Or I held on and he pulled away – we never could decide how it started. And I was destroyed again, and he was gone.

But in the times when we were separated, I was learning to live alone, and that was changing me. And although my life still felt like a really bad traffic accident, I was starting to enjoy asking myself that strange new question, 'What do *you* want to do, Liz?'

At first I was too worried about my divorce to think of answers. But then, slowly and quietly, an answer started to come. And every time it was the same: 'I want to learn to speak Italian.' I find the Italian language more beautiful than roses, and I had wanted to learn it for years. But it had never seemed sensible. Why learn Italian and not Spanish, which is spoken by millions of people in my own country? What could I do with Italian?

Now, though, in this dark time of my life, it was the only thing I could think of that would bring me any pleasure. That seemed a good enough reason. So I started learning Italian, and I loved it. After my evening classes, I came home and read Italian books in the bath, and the words made me laugh with happiness.

Also at this time, I found myself a spiritual teacher, or Guru. I had first seen her picture at David's apartment, and I knew at once – in my heart, not my head – that I wanted her to be my spiritual teacher. So the next Tuesday night, I went with David to a meeting in New York City, where this Guru's followers met every week to meditate and chant. That first night, when I came home, I felt light enough to run across every rooftop in the city. After that, I went to the chants every Tuesday, and I meditated every morning. And when I heard the Guru herself speak for the first time, and learned that she had an Ashram in India, I knew I must go there as soon as possible.

But before that, I had work to do. A women's magazine wanted to send me to Bali, in Indonesia, to write a story about yoga vacations. Bali is a very nice place – so how could anyone say no to that? While I was there, the yoga teacher took our group to visit a Balinese medicine man.

Ketut Liyer was a small old guy with happy eyes and almost no teeth. Our yoga teacher had told us that we could ask him about one question or problem we had, and I had been thinking about mine for days.

'Will you make my husband give me a divorce?' 'Will you make David fall in love with me again?' These were of course the questions I wanted to ask. But who travels around the world to meet an old medicine man in Indonesia and then asks about *boy trouble*?

'I want to have a real experience of God,' I decided at last to say. 'But I also want to enjoy the pleasures of this world.'

Ketut said he could answer my question with a picture. The picture he showed me was of a human, praying, but it had four legs, and no head. In the head's place, there were flowers, and near its heart, there was a small smiling face.

'This is how you will find the balance that you want,' said Ketut. 'You must have your feet strongly on the ground. But you must not look at the world through your head. You must look through your heart.' Then he asked me if he could read my palm.

'You like to travel,' he said, looking at my left hand. 'You will live a long time, and have many friends and many experiences. Your only problem is that you worry too much. You get good money for your work. You are someone who works with ideas. You will always get good money for this work you do. But one problem. You will lose all your money once in your life. Soon maybe, I think.'

'Very soon,' I said, thinking about my divorce.

'But you will get it all back again very quickly. You will have two marriages, one short, one long. And two children – no, one child – maybe – late in life. But there is something else.' He looked up at me, suddenly very sure about this. 'You will come back here to Bali one day. You must. You will stay for three, perhaps four months. Perhaps with my family. You will be my friend. I can learn better English

*Ketut Liyer, the Balinese medicine man,
reading my palm.*

with you. I think you are good with words. I think this work you do is something about words, yes?'

'Yes!' I said. 'I'm a writer. I'm a book writer!'

'So,' he said. 'You will come back here to Bali and teach me English, and I will teach you everything I know.'

'If you're serious, then I am,' I said.

He gave me a wide toothless smile and said, 'See you later.'

Now I'm the kind of person who, when a Balinese medicine man says you will come and live with him for four months, thinks you should do exactly that. And this was what gave me the idea to go traveling. How could I do it? I had to organize my divorce, I still had David-troubles, and I still had a magazine job that I couldn't just leave for three or four months. But I *had* to get back to Bali. The problem was, I wanted to visit my Guru's Ashram in India too. I had also been wanting for some time to go to Italy, so I could speak with real Italians, and live in a place where pleasure and beauty are important. So part of me wanted to eat spaghetti in Sorrento, and part of me wanted to wake up early every morning and spend the day meditating and praying. Which was most important? The truth was, as I had told Ketut Liyer, the medicine man, I wanted both. I wanted a balance of the good and the beautiful.

'Look at the world through your heart,' Ketut Liyer had said. So I stopped trying to choose between Italy, India, and Indonesia, and decided to travel to all of them. Four months in each place – a year's trip. I wanted to explore three different sides of myself, in places that have always done those things well. I wanted to explore pleasure in Italy, devotion in India, and, in Indonesia, how to balance those two things. I only noticed later that all three countries begin with the letter 'I'. How perfect, I thought, for a voyage to discover myself.

But I couldn't go anywhere until my divorce was organized. For months, my lawyer and my husband's lawyer had been trying to find an agreement. My husband wanted a lot of my money, but we were not now speaking to each other, and I just wanted to get out of the marriage. My lawyer had suggested a possible agreement to my husband, but would he sign it?

Every day I called my lawyer fourteen times, and every day she said the same thing. She was doing her best, and she would phone me at once if he signed. David and I had separated again, and this time it was final – or was it? We still couldn't let go completely. I had deep depression, and there were lines in my face from crying and from worry. I just wanted to end this useless argument between myself and my husband.

Then at last the call came. I was away for work in the middle of America, and I had been sleeping. I picked up the phone and whispered hello.

'Great news!' said my lawyer, from New York City, 2000 kilometers away. 'He just signed it!'

PART 1
Italy: Six Tales About the Search for Pleasure

—— 1 ——

A few weeks later, I am living in Italy.

I have left my job, got my divorce, moved out of my home, put everything I own in my sister's house, and packed two suitcases. My year of traveling has begun. And I can afford to do this because, amazingly, my publisher has bought the book I am going to write about my travels. It was just as the medicine man in Bali had said. I lost all my money and then got it back – or enough to buy me a year of life.

The first meal I ate in Rome was nothing much. Just some homemade pasta with a side plate of vegetables. Then the waitress brought me an extra plate for free – zucchini flowers with a soft bit of cheese in the middle (prepared so carefully that the zucchini flowers probably didn't even notice they weren't growing anymore). After the pasta I tried the meat. Oh, and I also drank a bottle of red wine, just for me. And ate some warm bread, with olive oil and salt.

I walked home after that meal to my apartment in an old building, not far from the Spanish Steps. I lay down in bed, turned off the light and waited to start crying or worrying, since that's what usually happened to me with the lights off. But I actually felt OK. I felt fine – almost happy.

'Was this all you needed then?' my tired body asked my tired mind. But there was no reply. I was already asleep.

Truthfully, I'm not the best traveler in the world.

First, I'm tall and fair and pink-faced, so I look wrong almost everywhere I go except Germany. I'm bad (or, actually, lazy) at finding out about a place before I go there. I'm not good at geography, and quite often I don't know exactly where I am. Also, when traveling in dangerous foreign places, it's useful to look calm, unworried, and completely in control all the time. I can't do that. When I'm confused or excited or afraid, I look confused or excited or afraid. And when I am lost, which is often, I look lost.

But still, traveling is the great true love of my life. I feel about travel the way a happy new mother feels about her newborn baby. I don't care about the sleepless nights, because I love it. Because it's mine.

Anyway, there are some things about me that are good for traveling. I am patient. I can pack light. I will eat anything. But the best thing is that I can make friends with anybody. This is why I'm not afraid to travel to places in the middle of nowhere. People asked me before I left for Italy, 'Do you have friends in Rome?' and I just shook my head, thinking to myself, 'But I will.'

Mostly when traveling, you meet your friends by accident. You sit next to them on a train, or in a restaurant. But a safer way is the 'letter of introduction'. So before I left for Italy, I asked everyone I knew in America if they had any friends in Rome, and I have arrived with a long list of names. The person on the list I most want to meet is a man named Luca Spaghetti. And yes, that really is his name.

First, though, I must start school. My classes begin today

at the Leonardo da Vinci Academy of Language Studies, where I am going to study Italian five days a week, four hours a day. There are twelve students, of all ages, and from all over the world, and everyone has come to Rome for the same reason – to study Italian just because they want to. A sad-faced Russian woman tells us she is having Italian lessons because 'I think I need something beautiful'.

I find out over the next few months that there are good reasons why Italian is the most beautiful language in the world. Until 1861, Italy wasn't even a country; it was a collection of different cities that were always at war with each other. And each city spoke a different local dialect. So for centuries, an Italian in Florence could not understand or speak to an Italian from Sicily or Venice. In the sixteenth century, some important Italian people got together and decided that Italy needed an Italian language. They chose the most beautiful of all the dialects – the language used by the poet Dante two hundred years earlier – and called it Italian. The Italian we speak today, therefore, is the language of fourteenth-century Florence, shaped and added to by one of the western world's greatest poets.

So it's not surprising that I want so desperately to learn this language.

—— 2 ——

Depression and Loneliness find me after about ten days in Italy. I am walking through the gardens near my apartment one evening after a happy day in school, and the sun is turning gold as it goes down over the church of St Peter's

Basilica. I am feeling happy, but I stop to watch the sun go down, and I start thinking a little too much, and that's when they find me.

Loneliness starts questioning me, which I hate because it always goes on for hours. He asks why I am all by myself tonight, again. He asks why I destroyed my marriage, why I destroyed my relationship with David, why I'm not at home living in a nice house and having nice children. He asks why I think I can enjoy a vacation in Rome when I've made such a disaster of my life.

I walk back home, hoping to lose them, but they follow me into my apartment. Depression gives me that dark smile, then sits in my favorite chair and puts his feet on my table. Loneliness watches, then climbs into my bed. He's going to make me sleep with him again tonight, I just know it.

I'd stopped taking my anti-depressants only a few days earlier. It had seemed crazy to be taking anti-depressants in Italy. How could I have depression here?

I'd never wanted to take anti-depressants. But during the last few years, there was no question that I had a serious depression. When you're lost in those woods, you sometimes don't realize at first that you *are* lost. For the longest time, you can tell yourself that you will find the path again any moment now. Then night comes again and again, and you have to accept that you are so far off the path that you don't even know where the sun is anymore.

I took on my depression like it was the fight of my life, which, of course, it was. I bought all the self-help books. I saw a therapist who was as kind as she was understanding.

*I stop to watch the sun go down, and I start thinking
a little too much.*

I prayed. I exercised. I kept myself away from sad movies, books, and songs. I spent as much time as possible with my family and closest friends.

But after two years of this battle, there was a night when I sat on the floor of my bedroom for many hours, trying very hard not to cut into my arm with a kitchen knife. The next morning I called my friend Susan, and I will never forget her face when she ran into my apartment and saw me there. Her fear for my life mirrored my pain, and it was terrifying. Susan made the phone calls and found a doctor who could see me that day. He asked me why I had taken so long to get help, and he gave me anti-depressants. Quickly, in less than a week, I could feel a little bit of daylight opening in my mind. Also, I could finally sleep.

Still, I never felt happy taking anti-depressants, though they helped immediately. I started taking them in January 2003, and by May I was already beginning to stop them.

But here I am. I am in Rome, and I am in trouble. Depression and Loneliness have pushed their way into my life again, and I took my last anti-depressants three days ago. So I pick up my most private notebook, which I keep in case I'm ever in emergency trouble, and I write:

'I need your help.'

After a while, the answer comes in my own writing:

I'm right here. What can I do for you?

And here begins again my strangest and most secret conversation. Here, in this most private notebook, is where I talk to myself. I talk to the same voice I met that night on my bathroom floor when I had first prayed to God for help.

In the years since then, I've found that voice again when I have been desperate, and I've learned that the best way for me to reach it is written conversation. Maybe the voice I am reaching for is God, or maybe it's my Guru speaking through me, or maybe it's all in my own mind.

What I write in my notebook tonight is that I am weak and full of fear. I explain that Depression and Loneliness are here again and I'm scared that they will never leave.

Then I find myself writing to myself:

I'm here. I love you, and I will always stay with you. I am stronger than Depression and I am braver than Loneliness, and nothing will ever exhaust me.

I fall asleep holding my notebook, and in the morning Depression has gone. Sometime during the night, he got up and left. And his best friend Loneliness went too.

—— 3 ——

I needed to make some friends. So I got busy with it, and now it is October and I have a nice group of them.

Sofie is my best friend from my language class. She is Swedish and in her late twenties, and very, very cute. She has just taken four months out from her good job in a Swedish bank, because she wanted to come to Rome and learn how to speak beautiful Italian. Every day after class, Sofie and I go sit by the river, eating ice cream and studying together.

I've also become friends with a couple called Maria and Giulio, who were introduced to me by an American friend. Maria is from America, Giulio is from the south of Italy. He doesn't speak great English, but she speaks very good

Italian. Giulio wants to learn English and asked if he could be another Exchange Partner for me. So we now meet for lunch twice a week to speak Italian and English.

But my newest best friend in Italy is, of course, Luca Spaghetti. Even in Italy, I've now learned, people think it's very funny to have a last name like Spaghetti. Luca speaks perfect English and is a good eater (in Italian, *una buona forchetta* – a good fork) so he's a great friend for hungry me. We spend a lot of time in dirty little restaurants with no name in the back streets of Rome. Homemade red wine. Great plates of pasta brought to us by proud, strong guys who are Roman through and through.

Luca has traveled quite a bit, but he says he could never live anywhere but in Rome, near his mother, since he is an Italian man. He's in his early thirties, and has had the same girlfriend for nearly twenty years. All his friends are the same friends he's had since he was a child, and all from the same part of Rome. They watch soccer matches every Sunday and then they all return separately to the homes where they grew up, to eat the big Sunday meals cooked by their mothers and grandmothers.

I wouldn't move from Rome, either, if I were Luca Spaghetti.

Sometimes, I must say, I wonder what I'm doing here.

I have come to Italy to experience pleasure, but I am not used to this kind of life. My parents have a small farm, and my sister and I grew up working. We had a lot of laughter in our house, but on all the walls there were lists of things to do, and I never experienced or saw laziness, not once.

Most Americans find it difficult just to enjoy pleasure. Ours is a country that looks for entertainment, but not really pleasure. Americans don't know how to do *nothing*. I once asked Luca Spaghetti if Italians have the same problem. He laughed so hard that he almost drove off the road.

'Oh no!' he said. 'We are the best in the world at *bel far niente.*'

Bel far niente means 'the beauty of doing nothing'. Italians are hard workers, but for them *bel far niente* is always the goal of all your work. The more wonderfully you can do nothing, the better you have done in life. So when I told my Italian friends that I'd come to their country to experience four months of pleasure, they didn't question it for a moment. 'Great!' they all said. 'Go on, enjoy yourself.'

During my first few weeks in Italy, I still couldn't quite let go. Then I realized that the only question I needed to ask was 'What, for me, is pleasure?' and everything changed. Everything became . . . delicious. I found that all I really wanted was to eat beautiful food and to speak as much beautiful Italian as possible. That was it.

—— 4 ——

My Exchange Partner Giovanni and I have a good time teaching each other expressions in English and Italian. We were talking one evening about what you say to someone who's very sad. You try to tell them that you understand because you've had a similar experience yourself, so you say, 'I've been there.'

'So sadness is a place?' Giovanni asked.

'Sometimes people live there for years,' I said.

So far, my favorite thing to say in all of Italian is a simple word: '*Attraversiamo*.'

It means 'Let's cross over.' Friends say it to each other when they're walking down the street and have decided to move to the other side. Giovanni can't understand why I like it so much. But to my ear, it has all my favorite Italian sounds. I love this word. I say it all the time now. I'm always pulling Sofie across the street through crazy Roman traffic.

This week I meet a young Australian girl who is traveling through Europe for the first time in her life. Something about meeting her just makes me want to go somewhere so much. I call Sofie and say, 'Let's go down to Naples for the day and eat some pizza!'

Immediately, just a few hours later, we are on the train, and then we are there. I love Naples at once. It is wild, noisy, dirty. In every street, there is some tough little kid screaming up at some other tough little kid on a rooftop. And in every building there's a bent old woman sat at her window looking down at it all.

The people here are so proud that they are from Naples, and why shouldn't they be? This is a city that gave the world pizza *and* ice cream. Giovanni is from Naples, and before I left Rome he gave me the name of the restaurant here that sells the best pizza. I find this wildly exciting, because the best pizza in Italy is from Naples, and the best pizza in the world is from Italy, which means this restaurant must make *the best pizza in the world!*

So Sofie and I have come to Pizzeria da Michele, and

I love my pizza so much that I have started to believe my pizza might actually love me back. I am having a relationship with this pizza, almost an affair. Sofie is nearly crying over hers, asking me, 'Why do they even try and make pizza in Sweden? Why do we even eat food at all in Sweden?'

Pizzeria da Michele is a small place, and by one o'clock the streets outside are full of people trying to get into it. They only have two kinds of pizza – regular and extra cheese. Sofie and I get another whole pizza each, and Sofie tries to calm down, but really, the pizza is so good we can't control ourselves.

When I look at myself in the mirror of the best pizza restaurant in Naples, I see a bright-eyed, clear-skinned, happy and healthy face. I haven't seen a face like that on me for a long time.

'Thank you,' I whisper. Then Sofie and I run out in the rain to look for cakes.

It is this happiness, I suppose (which is a few months old by now), that makes me think that it's time for David and me to end our story forever. We were already separated, but there was still a hope that perhaps some day we could try again. It's been so hard to imagine living a life without David. But something about my day in Naples has made me certain that I not only can find happiness without David, but must.

So I write him an email, and explain that I think we need to end this relationship completely.

I don't sleep much that night, imagining David reading my words. I run back to the Internet café a few times the

*I love my pizza so much that I have started to believe
my pizza might actually love me back.*

next day, looking for his reply. Part of me is desperate to find that he has replied: 'COME BACK! DON'T GO! I'LL CHANGE!' But around ten o'clock the next night, I finally get my answer. David agrees that yes, we really should say goodbye forever. He's been thinking the same thing himself, he says. He hopes that I know how much he loves me. 'But we are not what the other one needs,' he says.

I sit there staring at the computer screen for a long, sad time. Then my cell phone rings.

It's Giovanni. He says he's been waiting for me for over an hour in the pizza restaurant where we always meet on Thursday evenings to talk Italian and English.

I'd forgotten. I tell him where I am, and a few minutes later his little red car arrives and I climb in. He asks me what's the matter. I open my mouth to reply and start crying.

Poor Giovanni! He drives for a bit, then parks and waits for me to calm down. We have never had a conversation about our private lives, me and Giovanni. He does not even know that I am divorced or that I have left love behind in America.

He says, 'I'm sorry, but I don't understand. Did you lose something today?'

I take a deep breath and say: 'It's about a love story, Giovanni. I had to say goodbye to someone today.'

Then I start crying again. Giovanni sits quietly and waits until I've calmed down once more. Then, slowly and clearly and kindly, choosing each word carefully (as his English teacher, I was so *proud* of him that night), he says, 'I understand, Liz. I've been there.'

—— 5 ——

Over the next couple of months, I travel to Bologna, to Florence, to Venice, to Sicily, to Sardinia, once more down to Naples, then over to Calabria. These are short trips, mostly – a week here, a weekend there – just enough time to get the feel for a place, to look around, to ask people on the street where the good food is, and then to go eat it.

Florence is a weekend with my aunt and uncle, who have flown in from America to visit Italy for the first time in their lives, and to see me, of course. From there I go on alone to Lucca, where the best meat I've seen in all of Italy is laid out in shops across town. The town is famous, too, because Puccini was born here. I know I should be interested in this, but I'm much more interested in the secret a man in a shop told me – that you can get the best mushrooms in town in a restaurant across from Puccini's house. So I ask in Italian, 'Can you tell me where is the house of Puccini?' A kind person takes me right to it, and then is probably very surprised when I say *grazie* – thank you – and walk away into a restaurant across the street to eat mushrooms.

On the long train ride to Venice, I am sitting opposite a good-looking young Italian guy who sleeps for hours and wakes up shortly before we arrive. He looks me over carefully from foot to head, then says under his breath, '*Carina*.' Which means: cute.

'*Grazie mille*,' I tell him, with extreme politeness. A thousand thanks.

He's surprised. He didn't realize I spoke Italian. Neither did I, actually, but we talk for about twenty minutes and

I realize for the first time that I do. Some line has been crossed and I'm actually speaking Italian now. I'm not changing the words from English into Italian – I'm talking. Of course, there are lots of mistakes, but I can talk to this guy without trying too hard. He thinks I like him, but it's the words, not him, that are making me lovesick. He wants me to meet him later in Venice, but I have no interest in him. Anyway, I'm meeting my friend Linda in Venice.

I met Linda in Bali almost two years ago, and I invited her on this part of my trip because I refuse to go to the most romantic city on earth by myself, no, not now, not this year. Linda's one of my favorite traveling companions – funny, calm, and completely unable to understand depression. Her sunny nature, her brightness do not match this smelly, slow, quiet, strange city. Venice seems like a wonderful city for dying a slow death, or losing a loved one. Seeing Venice, I'm glad that I chose to live in Rome instead.

But I don't feel any depression here. I can even enjoy the melancholy of Venice, just for a few days. Somewhere in me I recognize that this is not my melancholy; this is the city's own melancholy. And this is a sign, I think, of me healing.

I get off the train a few days later in hot, sunny Rome, and it's nice to be back. The city is so awake and alive, so sexy in the sunshine. I remember my friend Giulio once asked me what I thought of Rome, and I told him that I really loved the place, of course, but I knew it was not my city, not where I'd live for the rest of my life.

Then he said, 'Maybe you and Rome just have different words.'

'What do you mean?'

Then he explained that the secret to understanding a city and its people is to learn its word. That there is one word for every city, and for most of the people who live there. And if your word doesn't match the word of the city, you don't really belong there.

'What's Rome's word?' I asked him.

'SEX,' he said. 'Everyone in Rome, all day, that is all they are thinking about.'

Now if you believe Giulio, that little word – SEX – is everywhere in Rome. Thinking about it, dressing for it, looking for it, refusing it, making a sport and game out of it – that's all anybody is doing. Which explains why Rome doesn't quite feel like my hometown. Not at this moment in my life. Because SEX isn't my word right now. It has been at other times in my life, but it isn't right now.

'What is your word?' Giulio asks me.

Now that, I could not answer. I've been thinking about it for a few weeks now, and I still can't answer it any better. I know some words that it definitely isn't. It's not MARRIAGE. It's not FAMILY, and it's not DEPRESSION anymore, thankfully. Over the last months in Italy, my word has mainly been PLEASURE, but that isn't all I am, or I wouldn't want to go to India so much. Perhaps my word is DEVOTION, but that doesn't match up with how much wine I've been drinking.

I don't know the answer, and I suppose that's what this year of traveling is about. Finding my word.

—— 6 ——

Luca Spaghetti's birthday is on America's Thanksgiving Day this year, so he wants, with my help, to cook an American meal for his birthday party. He says we can use the kitchen of his friends Mario and Simona, who have a nice big house in the mountains outside Rome, where he always has his birthday parties.

My friend Deborah has come to Rome from America for the weekend. Sofie is coming to Luca's party too, as well as Luca's girlfriend and some other friends. Everybody is always welcome on Thanksgiving, and even more because it is also Luca Spaghetti's birthday.

We drive out of Rome late in the evening, up into the mountains, and arrive at Mario and Simona's house. It's a beautiful house, hidden among olive and lemon trees. A fire is burning. The olive oil is homemade.

Luca had been worried about conversation at the party, because half the people can't speak Italian and the other half can't speak English, but it's one of those wonderful evenings where everyone understands each other perfectly.

Then Deborah suggests that we do something a lot of Americans like to do at Thanksgiving – join hands and say, one at a time, what we are most grateful for. Deborah starts, saying she is grateful that America will soon get to pick a new president. Sofie says (first in Swedish, then in Italian, then in English) that she is grateful for the kind hearts of Italy and for these four months she's been able to experience such pleasure in this country. Then Mario cries as he thanks God for his work, which has made it possible for him to have this beautiful home for his friends and family to enjoy.

When it is my turn, I find I cannot say my real thoughts: that I am grateful to be free tonight from the depression that had eaten away at me for years. Instead, I say a simpler truth – that I am grateful for old and new friends. That tonight, I am most grateful for Luca Spaghetti. That I hope he has a happy birthday, and lives a long life, so he can be an example to other men of how to be generous and loving. That I hope nobody minds that I am crying, but I don't think they do, because they are all crying too.

Luca almost cannot speak, and just says to us, 'Your tears are my prayers.'

Our party doesn't end until the sun is nearly coming up. Luca Spaghetti drives me and Deborah and Sofie all the way back home. We try to help him stay awake by singing Christmas songs. We sing again and again in every language we know as we all drive back into Rome together.

I have only a week left here, so – perhaps to prepare myself for my trip to India – I decide to travel through Sicily, the poorest part of Italy. When I arrive in the coastal town of Taormina, I find a sleepy policeman, and ask my favorite question in Italian: 'Where is the best food in this town?' He gives me one of the greatest things anyone can ever give me in life – a little piece of paper with the name of a restaurant written on it, where I eat the most amazing meal I've eaten yet in all of Italy. It's pasta, filled with hot, delicious seafood. Followed by rabbit cooked in some special Sicilian way.

But Syracuse, the next day, is even better. I love this town immediately. There are three thousand years of history under my feet in Syracuse. I ask a fisherman where I should eat, and he sends me to a little restaurant with no name, where, as soon as I sit down, the waiter brings me airy clouds of cheese, pieces of bread in sweet-smelling oils, plates of meat and olives, and a salad of cold oranges.

Is it so very bad to live like this for just a little while? Here in Sicily, which is terribly poor, it is difficult to forget about real life. But perhaps, in a place like this, thinking about your next wonderful meal is one thing that can keep you believing in yourself.

It was in a bath back in New York, reading Italian words aloud, that I first started healing myself. My life had gone to pieces, but I felt a little bit of happiness when I started studying Italian, and when you feel that, after such a dark time, you have to hold on and not let go until it pulls you out of the dirt. You were given life; you can and you must find something beautiful in it.

I came to Italy tired and thin. I did not know what I would find here. But I do know that, through enjoying pleasures, I have become a much more whole person. I am heavier, bigger than I was four months ago – a bigger person with a bigger life.

PART 2
India: Six Tales About the Search for Devotion

— 1 —

My plane lands in Mumbai around 1.30 a.m. It is December 30. I find a taxi that takes me hours out of the city to the Ashram, in a village far out in the countryside. I sleep on the drive through night-time India, sometimes waking to look out the window, where I can see thin women walking along the road carrying firewood on their heads. *At this hour?*

We arrive at the Ashram at 3.30 a.m., right in front of the temple, and a young man steps out of the shadows and introduces himself. He is Arturo, and he's here to welcome me. As we're making our whispered introductions, I can hear the beginning of my favorite Sanskrit hymn coming from inside. It's the morning *arati* – the first morning prayer – sung every day at 3.30 a.m. as the Ashram wakes. I look at the temple, asking Arturo, 'May I?' and he points inside. So I take off my shoes, kneel, and touch my head to the temple step. Then I go inside, joining the small group of mostly Indian women who are singing this beautiful hymn.

I know every word of this devotional song. The women finish singing, then move out of a door into a smaller temple. I follow them. The room is filled with people, Indian and Western, all seated in meditation. I go in beside them, put my hands on my knees, close my eyes.

I have not meditated, or even thought about meditating,

in four months. I say the mantra to myself once very slowly. *Om Namah Shivaya*. Then I say it again. Again. And again. I don't know if I fall asleep or how much time passes. But when the sun finally comes up that morning in India and everyone opens their eyes and looks around, Italy seems ten thousand miles away. I feel I have been here forever.

❀

'Why do we do yoga?'

I had a yoga teacher in New York once ask that question. Yoga, in Sanskrit, means 'union'. And what you have to do in yoga is find union – between mind and body, between a person and her God, between our thoughts and where they come from, between teacher and student, and even between ourselves and our neighbors. In the West, we mainly know yoga for its now-famous exercises for the body, but this is only one part of yoga. Yoga was first developed to get bodies and minds ready for meditation.

True yoga can be used by people of any religion. It's about experiencing God inside you and then holding on to that experience forever. It's about pulling your mind away from endlessly thinking about your past and worrying about the future. It's about searching for a place of perfect balance, both inside and outside yourself.

Like all great ideas, this one is simple to understand but almost impossible to take on. That is why in India everyone accepts that you need a teacher for your yoga – a Guru. This is someone who has found this balanced way of being and can help others to find it too.

If you're lucky enough, you will find a living Guru. It was

only one month after my first night of desperate prayer on my bathroom floor that I found mine. The first time I saw her, in that photograph in David's apartment, I felt she was saying, 'You called for me and now I'm here. So do you want to do this thing, or not?'

I must always remember what I replied that night: a simple and bottomless YES.

—— 2 ——

Outside the walls of the Ashram is a small village. It's a poor place, with one dirt street, one temple, a few shops, and a lot of cows. Inside the Ashram, it's gardens, flowers, birdsong, and beautiful trees. The buildings are nice, but simple. There's a dining hall, a big library of spiritual writing from the world's different religions, a few temples, and two dark rooms for meditation. There's an outdoor room where yoga classes are held in the morning and a park with a path around it where students can run for exercise.

Some people are paid to work at the Ashram, but most of the work here is done by the students. It's not a hotel or a vacation place. It's more like a university. You cannot come here unless you have been studying yoga for a long time, and you have to stay for one month. (I've decided to stay for six weeks, and then to travel around India on my own.)

Ashram life is tough. Days begin at 3 a.m. and end at 9 p.m., and you spend hours and hours a day in silent meditation, with little to take you away from the workings of your own mind. You live close together with people you don't know, in the Indian countryside. Sometimes it rains

*Inside the Ashram, it's gardens, flowers, birdsong,
and beautiful trees.*

hard for weeks, sometimes it is impossibly hot even before breakfast. Things can get deeply real around here, very fast.

My Guru always says that only one thing will happen when you come to the Ashram – that you will discover who you really are.

I have only one day to find my way around the Ashram, and then it is already New Year's Eve. After dinner, people come and sit outside. The Indian women are dressed in their best saris and gold bracelets, and we are going to chant until midnight, until the year changes. I'm tired from my journey, but the music and the singing carry me along. We sit cross-legged on the ground in the warm dark night, our bodies moving from side to side in time with the chanting. Then, at 11.30, the music gets faster, lifting the chant into happiness. Beautifully dressed women are dancing, and it feels like we are pulling the year 2004 toward us.

This is the first New Year's Eve I can ever remember in my life where I haven't known any of the people I am with. In all this dancing and singing, there is no one for me to hug at midnight. But I wouldn't say that anything about this night has been lonely. No, I would not say that at all.

❁

We are all given work here, and my job is to clean the temple floors. It's tiring work, but those hours spent cleaning are much easier than my hours of meditation. The truth is, I don't think I'm good at meditation. People say that prayer is talking to God, and meditation is listening. Well, I can talk to God all day about my problems, but when I try to be silent and listen, my mind quickly turns bored, angry, depressed, worried, or all of these. One of my many, many problems with meditation is that the mantra I have been given – *Om Namah Shivaya* – doesn't sit comfortably in my head. I love the sound of it and the meaning of it, but it does not help me meditate.

This morning, I arrive on time for the 4 a.m. meditation which always starts the day here. We have to sit for an hour in silence, but I count every minute, and by minute fourteen, my knees are hurting and I'm mad at myself. I fight against my mind, but it wins, my eyes fly open and I'm in tears. This is too much for me. I can't do it. My mind will not stop talking to itself, and I wonder how I'm ever going to control that machine in my head.

—— 3 ——

Dinnertime. I'm sitting alone, trying to eat slowly. My Guru always tells us to be strong with ourselves about food. She tells us to eat little and slowly. (My Guru, I'm pretty sure, has never been to Naples.) So I'm sitting at the dinner table trying to hold back my fork when Richard from Texas walks over. He's got a cool, no-big-hurry kind of walk. He's in his fifties, with white hair and a white beard, wide shoulders and big hands, but a completely relaxed face. He's not a guy who worries about a lot of things. But I am, and that's why I soon come to love him. His great confidence calms down all my worries and reminds me that everything really is going to be OK. (And if not OK, then at least funny.) 'Me and Groceries, we're laughin' the whole time,' says Richard.

Groceries. That's the name Richard gave me the first night we met, when he saw how much I could eat.

'What should I do about my meditation?' I ask Richard one day, as he's watching me clean the temple floors. (He likes watching me clean the floors. He thinks it's funny.)

'Why do you have to do anything about it, Groceries?'

'I can't get my mind to sit still.'

'Remember what the Guru teaches us – if you sit down to meditate, you can't control what happens next.'

'But all I do is argue with myself when I try and meditate.'

'Ever try to take a toy away from a little kid? Best way is to give him something else to play with. Don't try to take thoughts out of your mind – give your mind something better to play with. Something healthier.'

'Like what?'

'Like love, Groceries. God's love.'

So after that conversation with Richard, I try something new. I sit down to meditate and say to my mind, 'Listen – I understand you're a little frightened. But I promise, I'm just trying to give you a place to rest. I love you.'

I'm trying a different mantra, too. It's simple. *Ham-sa.* In Sanskrit it means 'I am That'.

Ham-sa.

I am That. I am with God, I am an expression of God, I am not separate, I am not alone. I am That.

Thoughts come, but I don't listen to them. I tell them to go away. I am busy, I am listening to God.

Ham-sa.

I am That.

I fall asleep for a while, I think. And when I awake, I can feel this soft blue light burning through my body. It's a little alarming, but amazing too. It gets bigger, faster, noisier, stronger. It's so strong now that it frightens me and I say to it, 'I'm not ready yet!' and open my eyes. It goes away. I'm back in the room again. I have been here – or somewhere – for almost an hour.

I am breathing very fast.

Kundalini shakti – the union of a human being with God. Religious people describe this strange, wild experience in many different ways. It usually happens during meditation, they say, when the mind is in a deep stillness. It can be dangerous to play around with *kundalini shakti*, and you need a teacher – a Guru – to help you experience it safely.

❀

For the last two nights, my mind has been full of terrible worries that I haven't felt since the worst of the divorce years. My thoughts keep flying back to my failed marriage. Worse, I'm thinking about David again. Why are all these things coming up again now?

I don't want anyone to talk to me, but Richard from Texas finds me at dinner and sits down – brave man – in my black smoke of self-hate.

'What's the matter with you?' he asks.

'Don't ask,' I say, but then I start talking and tell him everything, ending, 'And worst of all, I can't stop thinking about David.'

He says, 'Give it another six months, you'll feel better.'

'I've already given it twelve months, Richard.'

'Then give it six more. Groceries, listen to me. Some day you'll look back on this moment of your life. You're a strong woman, and normally you get what you want out of life, but in your last few relationships you didn't. Your problem is, you just can't let this one go. Well, you gotta learn how to let go, Groceries, or you're gonna make yourself sick.'

The next morning in meditation, all my old hateful thoughts come up again. But after an hour, I try a new idea. I try to be generous to myself. I stop thinking about failing, and try to accept that I am only a normal human being. Then the hateful emotions come up as usual, and I begin feeling lonely and angry.

My mind starts to argue, but suddenly a great voice shouts inside me. The voice comes from somewhere deep inside my heart, and it is like nothing I have ever heard before.

YOU HAVE NO IDEA HOW STRONG MY LOVE IS!!!

My thoughts and arguments run away, terrified. Silence follows. And in that silence, finally – I begin to meditate on (and with) God.

Richard from Texas likes to wait for me when I come out of the meditation room. He likes to see how exhausted I am after my battles with myself. But this morning I come out of the meditation room like a different person.

'Look at *you*!' Richard says. 'We need to celebrate. Come on, I'll buy you a drink in town.'

—— 4 ——

The biggest difficulty in my Ashram experience is not meditation, actually. It's what we do every morning before breakfast – a chant called the *Gurugita*. I love all the other chants and hymns of this yoga, but the *Gurugita* feels long, boring, deep, and noisy. It takes about an hour and a half – and this is after an hour of meditation and a twenty-minute chanting of the first morning hymn. The *Gurugita* is the reason you have to get up at 3 a.m. around here.

I've started missing it and doing other things with my morning, like writing in my diary, or taking a shower, or calling my sister. But when I try to go to the chant, it just makes me mad. I don't feel like I'm singing it, I feel like it's pulling me behind it.

A few days ago, I decided to get advice from my favorite teacher in the Ashram. We went for a walk in the gardens one night after dinner, and I told him how much I disliked the *Gurugita*, and asked if I could stop singing it.

He laughed, and said, 'You don't have to sing it if you don't want to. Nobody around here is ever going to make you do anything you don't want to do.'

'But people say it's an important spiritual thing to do.'

'It is. The *Gurugita* is very strong. It burns away the thoughts that make you unhappy. And I think it's probably having a good effect on you if you're experiencing these strong emotions while you're chanting it.'

'What should I do?'

'You have to decide for yourself. But my advice is that you chant the *Gurugita* while you're here. These things can be painful but they're also good for you.'

So I went to the chant the next morning, and the *Gurugita* kicked me down the stairs – or anyway, that's how it felt.

The next day was even worse. I told myself, 'It's only an hour and a half – you can do anything for an hour and a half.' But I felt so angry that I wanted to bite somebody.

This morning I woke up only minutes before the *Gurugita* was to begin. I washed, dressed, and – feeling so angry – went to leave my room. Then I found that Delia, my roommate, had left before me and locked me in. This was a perfect reason for not going to the *Gurugita*, I thought.

But then, without another second's thought, I found myself climbing out of the window. I dropped four meters to the ground, cutting my leg on something on the way down, and the only thought in my head was: *I have to get to the Gurugita*. I picked myself up, ran to the temple, and with blood running down my leg, I started to sing the *Gurugita*.

I sat there, singing and bleeding and thinking that I needed to find something – or somebody – that I could sing this hymn for, so I could find a place of real love inside me. Then I got it: *Nick*.

Nick, my sister's son, is an eight-year-old boy, thin, sensitive, and frighteningly intelligent. For him, life is never simple, and sometimes he can't sleep because he can't stop his mind. So I sang the *Gurugita* to Nick, to help him sleep. I filled the song with everything I wanted to teach him about life. When I noticed that I was crying, the *Gurugita* was over. The hour and a half was finished. It felt like ten minutes.

I walked to the front of the temple to give thanks to God, to love, to myself, to my Guru, and to Nick. Then I went into the meditation room, and sat for almost two hours.

After that, I never missed the *Gurugita* again. And an

amazing thing happened that afternoon. I told Delia, my room-mate, that she had locked me in. She was shocked. She said, 'I can't think why I did that. And I've been thinking about you – I had this terrible dream about you last night.'

'Tell me,' I said.

'I dreamt that you were on fire,' Delia said. 'I jumped up to try to help you, but there was nothing of you left.'

It was then that I decided to stay at the Ashram, and not move on after six weeks to travel all over India. Something was telling me it would be wrong to run off now, when so much was happening right here in this small place. As usual, Richard from Texas had the last word.

'Groceries, listen to your friend Richard. Stay here. You got the rest of your life for sightseeing. You're on a spiritual journey, baby. You got a personal invitation from God here – you really gonna turn that away?'

—— 5 ——

Richard from Texas was married once, too. He had two sons, both grown men now, both close to their dad. He isn't close to his ex-wife, but he's not worried about this, while for me, it breaks my heart. One of the hardest things about my divorce was that my ex-husband never forgave me for leaving. Even when I was happy or excited about something, I could never forget that for long. *I am still hated by him.*

I was talking about all this one day with my friends at the Ashram. When lunch ended, my newest friend, a guy from New Zealand who is also a writer, gave me a note. It said to meet him after dinner; he wanted to show me something.

*Richard from Texas had the last word. 'Groceries,
listen to your friend Richard. Stay here.'*

When we met, he told me to follow him, that he had a present for me. He led me to a building in the Ashram I'd never been inside before, unlocked a door, and took me up to a beautiful rooftop. Then he pointed to a tower and said, 'I'm going to leave you now. You're going to go up there. Stay up there until it's finished.'

'Until what's finished?' I asked.

My friend just smiled, and gave me a piece of paper. Then he left.

I climbed to the top of the tower. I was now standing at the tallest place in the Ashram, looking across at mountains and farmland. It was lovely up there, and the sun was going down. I opened the piece of paper my friend had given me. *How to find freedom*, it said. It told me to forgive my husband, forgive myself, and let him go.

Watch the stars come out, and let go. With all your heart, ask for God's kindness, and let go. When the past has gone from you at last, let go. Then climb down and begin the rest of your life. With great happiness.

I watched the sun go down and then lay on my back and watched the stars come out. I sang a little prayer in Sanskrit and repeated it every time I saw a new star.

I had been wanting for so long to have a conversation with my ex-husband. I wanted us to forgive each other. I lay up there, high above the world, and I was all alone. I started meditating, and after a time I knew what to do. I could talk to him right now. Here. On this rooftop in India.

So, still in meditation, I invited my husband to please join me here. Then I waited until I felt him arrive.

Much later I opened my eyes, and I knew it was over. Not just my marriage and not just my divorce, but all the unfinished empty sadness of it . . . It was over. I was free. I would still have thoughts and emotions about my ex-husband, but now, after my time on the rooftop, I had a place to put them.

—— 6 ——

Richard from Texas left today. I took the drive with him to the airport, and we were both sad.

'What am I gonna do when I don't have Liz Gilbert to kick around anymore?' he said. 'You've had a good experience at the Ashram, haven't you? You look all different from a few months back, like you threw out some of that sadness you've been carrying around.'

'I'm feeling really happy these days, Richard. You've helped me a lot.'

'Good girl. And Groceries? Move ahead with your life, will ya? Find somebody new to love some day. Don't just spend your life thinking of David or your ex-husband.'

'I won't,' I said. And I knew suddenly that it was true – I wouldn't. I could feel all this old pain of lost love and past mistakes leaving me.

On my ride back to the Ashram, after saying goodbye to Richard, I decide that I've been talking too much. (To be honest, I've been talking too much my whole life.) Being silent and being alone are both important in devotion. So now that Richard is gone, I'm going to make the rest of my stay a completely quiet experience. I'll eat my meals alone, meditate for endless hours every day, and clean the temple floors without a sound.

But the very next morning, I am called to the office, and the nice lady there tells me that my work is changing. I'm not going to clean floors anymore. There are going to be some retreats – weeks of prayer and meditation – at the Ashram this spring, for people from all over the world. My job will be to take care of these people during their stay. They will be in silence for most of their retreat, but I will be the one person they can talk to if they have problems.

'We need someone who is friendly and smiling all the time, who loves meeting people,' said the woman.

This is what always happens at the Ashram. You decide what you need to do, or who you need to be, and then something happens which immediately shows you how little you understood about yourself. It seems I have not quite yet understood one of the most important truths of this yoga: *God lives in you, as you.* To know God, you only need to stop being separate from God. But you just stay as you were made, in your natural character.

The goal of the retreats is the *turiya* state – a state of continuous happiness. Most of us, if only for two minutes in our lives, have experienced this at some time or another – a moment when everything, for no reason, is perfect. Everyone has come here to try and find the *turiya* state.

I spend the whole retreat in the back of the temple, watching everyone as they meditate in the half-dark and complete quiet. It is my job to make sure that everyone is comfortable, that no one is in trouble. Every day I can feel them going deeper into silence until the whole Ashram is full of their stillness. I hadn't meant to go into meditation at the same time, but I find myself lifted by their devotion. So it is probably not surprising that this is when it happens. One Thursday afternoon in the back of the temple, I suddenly leave my body, I leave the room, I step through time, and I go into a place of great peace. This place is God, which means that I am inside God. I am a part of God. I think, 'I want to hold on to this experience forever!'

It was those two little words *I want*! Immediately, I begin to fall back into my own small everyday world. The harder I try to hold on to the place of God, the faster I fall.

The retreat ends two days later, and everyone comes out of silence. I get so many hugs from people, thanking me for my help.

'Oh, no! Thank *you*,' I keep saying – because how can I thank them enough for lifting me to such a place?

In my last weeks at the Ashram, I have a lot of time alone. I spend about four or five hours a day in the meditation rooms. Sometimes I have amazing experiences of *kundalini shakti*, other times I just feel sweet, quiet happiness. The thoughts still come into my head and dance around, but they don't cause me trouble anymore.

Oh, and I've found my word. When my Italian friend Giulio told me that Rome's word is SEX, he asked me what my word was. I've been wondering about it ever since, and I saw it during my last week at the Ashram. I was reading some old book about yoga when I found a Sanskrit word *ANTEVASIN*. It means 'one who lives at the edge'. It was someone who had left their busy village and gone to live at the edge of the forest where the devotional leaders were. He was not a villager anymore, but neither was he spiritually complete. He lived where he could see both worlds, but he looked toward the unknown. And he studied.

I've spent so much time these last years wondering what I'm supposed to be. A wife? A mother? An Italian? A traveler? But I'm not any of these things, not completely. I'm an *antevasin* – a student on the ever-changing edge near the wonderful forest of the new.

I strongly believe that you can choose from any religion to move your spirit and find peace in God. You take whatever works from wherever you can find it, and you keep moving toward the light.

❀

My plane leaves India at four in the morning, and I decide not to go to sleep at all that night, but to spend the whole evening in one of the meditation rooms. I'm not really a late-night person, but something in me wants to stay awake for these last hours at the Ashram. I close my eyes and let the mantra come. Then I go down into my own stillness.

I don't know what tells me that it's time to go meet my taxi, after several hours of this stillness, but when I look at my watch, it's exactly time to go. I have to fly to Indonesia now. How funny and strange.

PART 3
Indonesia: Six Tales About the Search for Balance

—— 1 ——

I've never had less of a plan in my life than I do when I arrive in Bali. I don't know where I'm going to live, I don't know what I'm going to do. I have no friends in Indonesia, or even friends-of-friends. All I have is the name of an old Balinese medicine man – Ketut Liyer – who lives in a village just outside the town of Ubud. But I don't remember the name of the village.

But Bali is quite a simple place to get around. It's not a big island, and it's a popular tourist place. English is spoken here widely and happily. So I take a taxi to the town of Ubud, and find a small and pretty hotel.

Ubud is in the center of Bali, in the mountains, with rice fields all around, Hindu temples, and rivers cutting through the forests. Balinese painting, dance, and religious ceremonies are all still important here, and there are good restaurants and nice little bookstores.

I unpack my bags and decide to go for a walk, to look around this town I haven't seen for two years. But on my way out, I ask Mario, one of the guys at the front desk of the hotel, if he can help me find my medicine man.

Mario asks me to repeat the name, and this time I write it down. At once, Mario's face brightens.

'Ketut Liyer! Ketut Liyer is famous healer.'

'Yes! That's him!'

I say, 'Hey, Mario – do you think you could take me to visit Ketut Liyer some day? If you're not too busy?'

'Not now,' he says. 'But in five minutes?'

So, on the same afternoon I arrive in Bali, I'm suddenly on the back of a motorbike, driving through the rice fields towards Ketut Liyer's home. When we arrive, I recognize the place at once. Inside a high stone wall there are several small homes joined together, with a temple at the back. We go inside, and there is Ketut Liyer, the old medicine man, looking exactly the same as he did when I first met him.

Mario says something to Ketut, and he turns his smile upon me, his face full of kindness, and shakes my hand.

'I am very happy to meet you,' he says.

He has no idea who I am. I tell him that I have been here to see him already, two years ago.

He looks confused. 'Not first time in Bali?'

'No, sir. I don't think you remember me, Ketut. I was here two years ago with an American yoga teacher. I asked for your help because I wanted to get closer to God. You drew me a picture.'

'Don't remember,' he says.

This is bad news – so bad it's almost funny. What am I going to do in Bali now? I'd been afraid of learning that he was dead, but I never thought he wouldn't remember me.

So I describe the picture he had made for me, with the four legs, no head, and the face in the heart. Then, getting desperate, I say, 'I could give you English lessons, you said. And you would teach me the things that you know.'

He listens to me politely, smiling and shaking his head.

'YOU!' *Ketut Liyer says.*
'*I remember YOU!*'

I try one last thing. I say, 'I'm the book writer, Ketut. I'm the book writer from New York.'

And for some reason that does it.

'YOU!' he says. 'I remember YOU!' He takes my shoulders in his hands and shakes me happily.

'You came back! You came BACK!'

I'm all tearful now, but trying not to show it. Even I am surprised by how deeply glad I am that he remembers me.

'I so happy!' he says. He's wildly excited now. 'I do not remember you at first. So long ago we meet! You look different now! Last time, you sad-looking woman. Now – so happy! Like different person!'

'Yes, Ketut. I was very sad before. But life is better now. Do you still want me to help you with your English, Ketut?'

He tells me I can start helping him right now. He goes into the house and comes back with letters he's had from abroad over the last few years. He asks me to read the letters to him; he can understand English well, but can't read much. I'm his secretary already. I'm a medicine man's secretary!

When the letters are finished, he tells me about recent changes in his life. Now he has a wife, for example. He points across at the large woman who's been standing near the kitchen door, staring at me like she wants to shoot me. Last time I was here, Ketut had sadly shown me photos of his wife who had recently died.

He says, 'You come to my house every day to help me with my English now?' I agree happily, and he says, 'I will teach you Balinese meditation, OK?'

'OK,' I say.

'I am very happy to meet you,' he says, shaking my hand.

I give him my first English lesson. I explain that we only say 'Nice to meet you' the first time we meet somebody. After that, we say 'Nice to see you'.

He likes this. He tries it out: 'Nice to see you! I am happy to see you!'

We shake hands, and agree that I will come again tomorrow afternoon.

'If you have any Western friend come to Bali, send them to me for palm-reading – I am very empty now in my bank. I am very happy to see you, Liss!'

'I am very happy to see you too, Ketut.'

—— 2 ——

Bali is a very small Hindu island in the middle of Indonesia, a very big Muslim country, and it has one of the most organized social and religious systems in the world. Everyone in Bali is in a clan, everyone knows which clan he is in, and everyone knows which clan everyone else is in. Religious ceremonies are very important, and most Balinese women spend a large part of their day preparing for, making, or cleaning up after a ceremony.

In Bali, everyone knows where he or she belongs. The Balinese understand all about balance, and I had hoped to learn a lot from them. But their way of thinking is very different from my Western way of thinking, and I realize that, to the Balinese, I am very far from being balanced. I travel around the world without knowing where I really am, and I have stepped away from marriage and family.

And if you don't know where you are or whose clan you belong to, how can you possibly find balance?

When you are walking down a road in Bali, the first question someone will ask you is, 'Where are you going?' and the second is, 'Where are you coming from?' They want to put you 'on the map'. The third question they will ask is, 'Are you married?' They really want you to say yes, so they know that your life is well organized. And if you have had a divorce, it is definitely best not to talk about it. It just makes the Balinese so worried.

⚕

In the morning, Mario helps me buy a bicycle, and in the afternoon I ride down into Ketut's village. There are people there when I arrive – a small family from the countryside who have brought their baby girl to Ketut for help. The poor little baby has teeth coming and has been crying for several nights. Ketut listens carefully as the parents explain their baby's troubles. Then he pulls out one of his old books, looks through it, and writes down for the parents what the baby needs. He puts water in a bowl, reads a mantra above it, and then blesses the baby with it.

Ketut Liyer is with this family for forty minutes, and they can only pay him about twenty-five cents. If they had no money at all, he would still do the same thing. He gets about ten visitors a day like this. On important religious days, when everyone wants a special blessing, he sometimes has more than one hundred visitors.

A few more people come in the afternoon, but Ketut and I have some time alone together too. He gives me my first lesson in Balinese meditation. He says many kinds of meditation are too difficult for Westerners, so he will teach me an easy one. Which is: sit in silence and smile. I love it.

'You can do yoga,' he says, 'but yoga too hard. To meditate, only you must smile. Smile with face, smile with mind. Try tonight at hotel.'

I am so free here in Bali. I meditate every morning as my Guru taught me, and in the evening I do Ketut's meditation. I visit Ketut for a few hours in the afternoon. The rest of the day, I walk around and ride my bike, eat lunch and sometimes talk to people. I found a quiet little library in the town, and now I spend lovely big parts of my day reading in the garden. After the hard work of devotional life in the Ashram, and even after the pleasures of eating in Italy, this is a new and wonderfully peaceful time in my life.

In the evenings I take my bicycle high up into the hills and through the rice fields, with views so lovely and green. A few nights ago, I found a small house for rent, up above the forest, and three days later I am living there. It has a bright red kitchen, a pond full of goldfish, and an outdoor shower, so I can watch the birds in the trees while I wash. Little secret paths go through a beautiful garden. There is so much beauty around here, it is almost difficult to believe. I can pick bananas off the trees outside my bedroom window. And the rent is less than I used to pay for taxis in New York every month.

Every day I ask Ketut if he really wants me at his home, and he always says I must come and spend time with him. Tonight, when the last of his patients has gone, and Ketut is exhausted, I ask if I should go now and he replies, 'I always have time for you.' Then he asks me to tell him some stories about India, about America, about Italy, about my family. That's when I realize that I'm not Ketut Liyer's English teacher, or his meditation student, but I'm that simplest of things for this old medicine man – I'm his friend. I'm somebody he can talk to because he likes hearing about the world and he hasn't had much chance to see it.

Things were not so easy with Ketut's wife Nyomo at first, though. She used to stare at me from inside her kitchen, and when I smiled, she would just keep staring.

But then something changed, after what happened with the notebooks. Ketut Liyer has lots of old notebooks, filled with writing about healing. He wrote these notes back in the 1940s or 1950s, and they are about everything he learned from his father, grandfather, and great-grandfathers, who were all medicine men. So they are extraordinarily valuable. There are books about medicines from trees and leaves and plants, palm-reading pictures, and more notebooks full of mantras and figures. The only thing is, these notebooks are falling to pieces.

'Ketut,' I said to him last week, holding up one of his old notebooks, 'I'm not a doctor like you are, but I think this book is dying.'

Then I asked if I could take the notebook into town with me and photocopy it before it died. I had to promise that I would only keep the notebook for twenty-four hours and that I would not damage it. Finally he let me take it, and I rode into town and carefully photocopied every page.

I brought the old and the new copies of the book back the next day, and Ketut was delighted.

I asked if I could photocopy the rest of his notebooks, and by the end of the week, several of them were done. Every day, Ketut called to his wife and showed her the new copies. The expression on her face didn't change at all, but she looked at the notebooks very closely.

The next Monday when I came to visit, Nyomo brought me hot coffee, for the first time. The next day she brought me coffee and sugar, and then, yesterday, I was standing saying goodbye to Ketut, and she came past behind me. My hands were behind my back, and she took one of them quietly and held it for a moment. Then she dropped it and walked away, saying not a single word.

—— 3 ——

The next day, I got hit by a bus, which knocked me off my bicycle. My bicycle was fine, but I had a deep cut on my knee that became nastily infected. I showed the cut to Ketut Liyer, who said, 'Infect. Nasty. You should go see doctor.'

This was a little surprising. Wasn't *he* the doctor? Perhaps he doesn't give medicine to Westerners. Or perhaps he had a secret plan, because it was my knee that caused me to meet Wayan. And from that meeting, everything happened.

Wayan Nuriyasih, like Ketut Liyer, is a Balinese healer. She's a woman in her thirties, and makes medicines in her own shop in the center of Ubud. I'd ridden past it many times. So when Ketut told me to see a doctor, I went there on my bike.

Wayan Nuriyasih, like Ketut Liyer,
is a Balinese healer.

Wayan's place is a small doctor's room and home and restaurant all at the same time. I went in and introduced myself to Wayan the healer – a beautiful Balinese woman with a wide smile and long black hair. There were two shy young girls hiding behind her in the kitchen. I showed Wayan my infected knee, and soon she was making me a medicinal drink and putting hot green leaves on the cut.

We got to talking. Her English was excellent, and because she is Balinese, she immediately asked, 'Are you married?'

When I told her I wasn't married, she looked surprised.

'Never been married?' she asked.

'No,' I lied.

'Really never been married?' she asked again.

OK, so she knows.

'Well,' I said, 'just once.'

Her face cleared. 'Divorced?' she asked.

'Yes,' I said, ashamed now.

'Me, too,' said Wayan, to my surprise. 'Me too, divorced.'

'*You?*'

'I did everything I could,' she said, and her eyes filled with tears. 'I try everything, praying every day. But I had to go away from him.'

Next thing I knew, I was holding Wayan's hand, saying, 'I'm sure you tried everything.' I stayed in the shop for the next five hours, talking with my new best friend about her troubles. Wayan's husband, she told me, was a man who drank all the time, then hit her when she didn't give him more money. She had to go to hospital several times, and she lost the baby she was carrying, her second child, after he hit her very badly one time. After which their first child, a bright little girl called Tutti, said, 'I think you should get a divorce, Mommy. Every time you go to the hospital you leave too much work around the house for Tutti.'

The Balinese family group is everything in Bali. Big families live together in a group of houses around the family temple, taking care of each other until death. Getting out of a marriage here leaves a person terribly alone. Wayan decided to save her own life and leave, which left her with nothing. But she did get her daughter, although she had to sell everything she owned in order to pay the lawyer.

For the last few years now, Wayan and Tutti have been living on their own, moving from place to place as the money comes and goes. As Wayan is telling me this story, Tutti herself comes running into the shop, home from school. She's eight years old now, full of character and fire, and she asks in English if I'd like to eat lunch.

'I forgot!' says Wayan. 'You should have lunch!' and the mother and daughter go into their kitchen and bring me, some time later, the best food I've had yet in Bali.

Little Tutti brought each part of the meal with a big smile, telling me in a bright voice what was on the plate.

I finally said, 'Tutti, where did you learn to speak such good English?'

'From a book!' she said.

'I think you are a very clever girl,' I told her.

'I show you my books!' Tutti sang, and she ran upstairs to get them. Already, after just one afternoon, I was so in love with this kid.

Before I left, Wayan took the green leaves off my leg, and felt both my knees. She smiled at me and said, 'I can feel from your knees that you don't have much sex lately. How long since sex for you?'

'About a year and a half.'

'You need a good man. I will find one for you. I will pray at the temple for a good man for you, because now you are my sister.'

So now I spend my mornings with Wayan at her shop, laughing and eating. I spend my afternoons with Ketut the medicine man, talking and drinking coffee. I spend my evenings in my lovely garden, reading. And every morning, I meditate while the sun comes up over the rice fields.

I came to Indonesia to search for balance, but after only a few weeks, I don't feel like I'm searching for anything anymore. The balance has just come naturally. I can feel my own peace, and I love the way I spend part of my day in devotion and part of it enjoying the pleasures of beautiful countryside, dear friends, and good food. I've been praying a lot lately, comfortably and often, and most of my prayers are thanks for the fullness of my happiness. I have never felt fewer troubles from myself or from the world.

—— 4 ——

A Brazilian friend of Wayan's invited me to a party tonight so I got out my only nice dress from the bottom of my bag and put it on. The dinner was great fun. I even got a little bit drunk, which felt strange after my months of praying at the

Ashram and drinking tea in my Balinese flower garden. And I was flirting! I hadn't flirted for a long time. But I wasn't really sure who I was flirting with. Was it the Australian sitting next to me? Or the quiet German down the table? Or was it the handsome older Brazilian man who had cooked this great meal for all of us? (I liked his kind brown eyes, and the way he spoke English. And his cooking, of course.)

The Brazilian food was amazing. I ate plate after plate. And then we went out dancing at a local bar, and on to a restaurant. I could not believe I was still awake at 3.30 a.m., and not to meditate, either! I was up in the middle of the night and wearing a dress.

Felipe, the handsome older Brazilian man, offered me a ride home.

'You're going to have a wonderful few months here in Bali. You wait and see.'

'I can't go out a lot, Felipe. I only have this dress. People will start to notice that I'm wearing the same thing all the time.'

'You're young and beautiful, darling. You only need the one dress.'

⚹

Today I am back in Wayan's restaurant, eating her delicious lunch special. She has just heard that her rent will go up in three months. She will probably have to move again because it will be too expensive for her. But she has very little money, and if they move, Tutti will have to change schools again. They need a home – a real home.

Where will Wayan go? Her own family are rice farmers

in the countryside and poor. If she goes and lives with them, her patients won't be able to reach her.

I have learned something else about Wayan. Those two shy girls I noticed on the first day, hiding in the back of the kitchen? They have no parents. Wayan found them begging in the market a few months ago, and they hadn't eaten for days. She took them home and now she cares for them like she cares for her own Tutti.

Today, as I was eating my lunch, I noticed that Tutti was doing something rather strange. She was walking around the shop with a small blue tile, whispering to it, singing to it. Finally she sat on it in a quiet corner, eyes closed.

I asked Wayan what this was all about. She said that builders had been working on a grand hotel down the road, and Tutti had found the tile outside, and had brought it home. She had said to her mother, 'If we have a house some day, it can have a pretty blue floor, like this.' Now, Wayan said, Tutti often sits on that tile for hours, shutting her eyes and pretending she's inside her own house.

When I heard that story, I thought, 'OK, that does it.'

I walked out of Wayan's shop, and went and wrote an email to all my friends and family across the world. I told everyone that my birthday was coming up in July. I told them that there was nothing in this world that I needed or wanted, and that I had never been happier in my life. And I asked if, instead of giving me birthday presents, they could give some money to help a woman named Wayan Nuriyasih buy a house in Indonesia for herself and her children.

Then I told the whole story of Wayan and Tutti and the

shy little girls. I promised that I would double the money my friends and family agreed to give.

By the next morning, people had already promised $700.

Then the email started to go around the world. Friends and family and generous people I didn't even know – they all gave money. Just seven days after I sent my email, I had almost $18,000 to buy Wayan Nuriyasih a home.

—— 5 ——

I don't want to tell Wayan about it, not until I have all the money. So for the whole week, I keep my mouth shut about my plans, and I keep myself busy having dinner almost every night with Felipe the Brazilian. He's more than he seems, this guy who knows everyone in Ubud and is always the center of the party. He's fifty-two years old, which is interesting. I like him, though. His eyes are warm and brown. He has a gentle face and he smells wonderful.

He's been living in Bali for about five years, making jewelry to sell in America. I like the fact that he was married for twenty years before his marriage broke down. I like the fact that he has grown-up children, and that they love him. I like that he speaks four languages. I like the way he listens to me, and I like being called 'my lovely little darling'.

He said to me the other night, 'Why don't you take a lover while you're in Bali, Liz?'

'I don't think I'm ready for it,' I say. 'I'm not even sure I know how to do it anymore. I think I was more confident about sex and love when I was sixteen than I am now.'

'Of course you were,' Felipe said. 'You were young and

stupid then. Only the young and stupid are confident about sex and love. Do you think any of us know what we're doing? Love is always difficult. But still humans must try to love each other, darling. It's a good sign, having a broken heart. It means we have tried for something.'

We talk about our marriages, our divorces. We talk about the bottomless depression that comes after a divorce. We drink wine and eat well together.

He says, 'Do you want to do something with me this weekend?' And I say yes, that would be nice. Because it *would* be nice.

⚕

I finally sat down with Wayan and told her about the money for her house. She was so shocked I had to sit with her for a few hours, telling her the story again and again, until she started to believe it.

The first thing she said was, 'Please, Liz, you must explain to everyone that this is not Wayan's house. This is the house of everyone who helped Wayan.'

Then she realized she was going to be able to have a garden, and she started to cry.

Slowly, happy thoughts started to come to her. If she had a home, she could have a small library for all her books! And a real restaurant with chairs and tables! If she had a home, Tutti could have a birthday party some day!

We went together to Wayan's little bank, and arranged the money, and then we returned to the shop and found Tutti just home from school. Wayan dropped to her knees, held Tutti and said, 'A house! A house! We have a house!'

*We talk about our marriages, our divorces. We drink wine
and eat well together.*

—— 6 ——

I went out with Brazilian Felipe again, twice over the
weekend. On Saturday I brought him to meet Wayan and the
kids, and I also brought him to meet Ketut, my medicine
man. Ketut read his palm and said seven times (looking hard
at me) that he was 'a good man, a very good man, a very very
good man. Not a bad man, Liss – *a good man.*'

Then on Sunday, Felipe asked if I'd like to spend a day at
the beach. I'd been in Bali for two months already and had
not yet seen the beach, so I said yes. He drove me to a hidden
little beach, with blue water and white sand, and we talked
all day, stopping only to swim and sleep and read. Then,
when it was dark, we walked arm-in-arm through the old
Balinese fishing village, under the stars. That's when Felipe
from Brazil asked me in the most relaxed way, 'Should we
have an affair together, Liz? What do you think?'

I liked everything about the way this was happening.
Not with a kiss, or a touch – but with a question.

I said, 'I would probably say yes, Felipe, normally.
Whatever normally is.'

We both laughed. But then I showed him why I was
hesitating. Because some great change is happening in my
life, and something inside me wants to keep the whole of
this year of traveling to myself. Because I don't want to lose
control of my life again.

Of course Felipe said that he understood, and that I
should do whatever's best for me. But he also wanted to
give his opinion.

'First, if I understand you correctly, this whole year is

about your search for the balance between devotion and pleasure. I can see there's been a lot of devotion, but I'm not sure where the pleasure has come in.'

'I ate a lot of pasta in Italy, Felipe.'

'Pasta, Liz? *Pasta*? Also, I think I know what you're worried about. Some man is going to come into your life and take everything from you again. I won't do that to you, darling. I don't want us to take anything from each other. It's just I've never enjoyed being with someone so much before, and I'd like to be with you.'

'Felipe,' I said, 'that's the most romantic offer a man has ever made me.'

And it was. But I still said no.

So I was surprised the next night when – after he'd made me dinner at his house and we'd sat talking for several hours – Felipe finally put his hand against my face and said, 'That's enough, darling. Come to my bed now,' and I *did*.

Yes, I did come to his bed with him, in that bedroom with its big open windows looking out over the night-time and the quiet Balinese rice fields.

The white curtain around Felipe's bed looked to me like a parachute. I felt I had been in an airplane which had been flying me out of A Very Hard Time in My Life. But I had stepped out of the airplane, and this white parachute carried me down through a strange empty place between my past and my future. And my safe landing was this small, bed-shaped island, with a handsome Brazilian who could only repeat these five words every time he looked at my face: *beautiful, beautiful, beautiful, beautiful, and beautiful.*

We didn't sleep at all, of course. And then, I had to *go*. I had to go back to my house stupidly early to meet my friend Yudhi. He and I had planned a week's road trip across Bali together, and we were leaving this morning.

So, for the next week, Yudhi and I drove across Bali, and every day I called Felipe and he asked, 'How many more sleeps until you come back to me?'

When we returned to Ubud, I went straight back to Felipe's house and we spent every minute of the next month together. I had never been loved like this before by anyone. He said, 'Darling, you're going to get bored of how much I love you, and how many times a day I tell you how beautiful you are.'

Try me, mister.

Wayan needs to buy a house, and I'm getting worried that it's not happening. Felipe and I have found someone who can take us around and show us houses, but Wayan hasn't liked anything we've seen.

I say to her, 'Wayan, it's important that we buy something. I'm leaving here in September, and I need to tell my friends that their money went into a home for you.'

'Not so simple to buy land in Bali,' she tells me. 'Can take a long time.'

'We don't have a long time, Wayan.'

But land in Bali is more expensive than I had thought, and everyone in Ubud has a story about the problems of trying to buy here. Also, Wayan has to look at the *taksu* – the spirit – of each place.

Last week Felipe found a place that seemed perfect, but when I asked Wayan, 'Should we buy it?' she replied, 'Don't know yet, Liz. I need to go to temple, pray, first.'

⚘

The land Felipe had found for Wayan doesn't happen. I'm getting really worried about this now. 'Wayan,' I tell her, 'I have to leave Bali in less than two weeks and go back to America. I can't tell my friends, who gave me all this money, that you still don't have a home.'

But a few days later, Wayan comes to Felipe's house, excited. She's found a different piece of land. It's close to town, it has good *taksu*, and she really loves it. I love this land, Felipe loves this land, Tutti loves it too.

'Buy it,' I tell Wayan.

But a few days later, she changes her story. The farmer who owns the land doesn't want to break it up. He wants to sell her a bigger piece of land, so she needs more money.

'Is she playing around with me?' I ask Felipe.

'Darling,' he says kindly. 'Of *course* she's playing around with you. But just because that's what everyone does here. She wants all the land, and she wants you to buy it for her. You must not think that she's not a good person. But you cannot let her use you. You need to control this.'

So the next day, I walk into Wayan's shop. I pretend that I am very worried.

'Wayan,' I say. 'We need to talk. I have a big problem. My friends in America are very angry with you.'

'With me? Why?'

'Because four months ago, they gave you a lot of money

to buy a home, and you did not buy a home yet. They think you are stealing their money, using it for something else.'

'I'm not stealing!'

'I know that, Wayan. This is why I'm so worried. I try to tell my friends in America that you are an honest person, but they don't believe me. They say that if you don't buy some land in the next week, then I must . . . *take the money back*.'

Wayan looks like she's going to die.

'Believe me, I find land now, don't worry, very fast I find land.'

'You must, Wayan,' I say. 'I'm going back to Felipe's house now. Call me when you've bought something.'

Four hours later – just four hours! – the phone rings in Felipe's house. It's Wayan. She has just bought the small piece of land from the farmer, and workers will start building her house next week – before I leave. She hopes that I am not angry with her. She wants me to know that she loves me more than she loves this whole world.

I tell her that I love her, too. And that I can't wait to visit her some day in her beautiful new home.

When I get off the phone, Felipe says, 'Good girl.' Then he says, 'Can we go on vacation now, please?'

※

The place we go to on vacation is a very small island called Gili Meno, near Lombok. The island of Gili Meno is one of the most important places in the world to me. I came here by myself two years ago – when I was in the very worst part of my dark journey through divorce. I came here to have ten days alone and in silence. I cried a lot, I prayed a lot, and I looked at all the sad and angry thoughts in my mind, accepted them, and took them into my heart.

Now I'm coming back to Gili Meno in very different times. Since I was last here, I've gone around the world, organized my divorce, separated from David, learned to speak a new language, sat in God's hand in India, studied at the feet of an Indonesian medicine man and bought a house for a family who needed a place to live. I am happy and healthy and balanced. And yes, I am also sailing to this pretty little island with my Brazilian lover.

I think about the woman I have become lately, and about the life that I am now living. And I think about how much I always wanted to be this person and live this life. I think of everything I went through before getting here and wonder if it was me – this happy, balanced me – who pulled the other younger, more confused me forward during all those hard years.

Felipe wakes up. We have been sleeping in each other's arms on this Indonesian fisherman's boat all afternoon. He tells me that he had an idea while he was sleeping.

He says, 'You know – I need to live in Bali because my work is here and it's close to Australia, where my kids live. I also need to be in Brazil often, and you need to be in the United States, because that's where your work is, and where your family and friends are. So I was thinking . . . perhaps we can build a life together around America, Australia, Brazil, and Bali.'

I can only laugh, because – why not? A life like this would seem crazy for some people, but it's just like me. And after

'Attraversiamo.'

a year of exploring the 'I's, Felipe has just suggested to me a whole new idea for traveling: Australia, America, Bali, Brazil = A, A, B, B.

The little fishing boat arrives at Gili Meno. There's nowhere to land a boat on this island. You have to jump off and walk through the water, getting really wet. But it doesn't matter, because the beach here is so beautiful, so special. So me and my lover, we take off our shoes and get ready to jump over the edge of that boat together, into the sea. But before we jump I say to Felipe, '*Attraversiamo.*'

Let's cross over.

GLOSSARY

affair (love affair) a sexual relationship between two people

amazing very surprising, in a pleasing way

anti-depressant medicine used to help people with depression

Ashram a place where Hindus live together as a group away from other people, studying, praying, and meditating

balance (*n*) having the right amount of each different thing

beg to ask for something because you want or need it very much

bless to ask God to keep someone or something safe

ceremony a formal public or religious event

chant (*v & n*) to sing or say a religious song or prayer, by repeating a few notes many times

clan a group of families who are related to each other

cute (*American English*) nice-looking

depression an illness when a person feels very sad and worried

devotion deep feelings of belief in a religion

dialect the way a language is spoken in one place, with different words, grammar, and pronunciation

divorce the ending by law of a marriage

emotion a strong feeling, like love, anger, or being afraid

entertainment something that makes you interested or amused

exercise (*n & v*) activities that you do to stay healthy

explore to learn more about something by looking at it carefully

flirt (*v*) to behave in a way that makes someone think you are interested in them sexually

forgive (somebody) to stop feeling angry with someone who has hurt you or made you sad

groceries food and other things you buy for the home; in this story used by Richard as a funny name for Elizabeth Gilbert

Guru a Hindu religious teacher or leader

healing getting better after an emotional shock
hold on to keep holding something
Hindu a person who follows Hinduism, the main religion of India
hug (*v & n*) to put your arms around someone and hold them, to show that you love them
hymn a religious song
infected containing bacteria that can make you ill
jewelry rings, bracelets, necklaces, earrings, etc.
magnificent doing great things; beautiful
mantra a word or sound that is repeated again and again
medicine man a person who, it is believed, has special powers to make sick people well again
meditate to think deeply, usually in silence, especially for religious reasons; **meditation** (*n*)
melancholy deep feeling of sadness
mind (*n*) the part of a person that makes them think and feel
mushroom a plant you can eat, with a round flat head
olive a small green or black fruit used in cooking and for its oil; **olive oil** oil made from olives
palm (read someone's palm) to say what you think will happen to someone by looking at the lines on their palm (the inside of the hand)
parachute a large piece of thin cloth that makes someone fall slowly when they are dropped from an airplane
partner the person that you are married to or having a sexual relationship with; a person that you do something with
pasta an Italian food made from flour, eggs, and water
photocopy to make a photographic copy of a paper
pleasure feeling or being happy
pray (*v*) to speak privately to God; **prayer** (*n*) speaking to God
Puccini an Italian musical composer, who wrote famous operas
relationship a loving and/or sexual friendship

relaxed calm and not worried

religion (*n*) belief in a god or gods; **religious** (*adj*) about religion

rent money that you pay every week or month for using a house

romantic about love or a sexual relationship

Sanskrit an ancient language of India; Hindu religious texts are written in Sanskrit

separation when a husband and wife stop living together

sex (*n*) a physical relationship between two people; **sexy** (*adj*) exciting and interesting in a sexual way

shocked surprised and upset

social the way people live together in groups, villages, and towns

spiritual religious

system the laws or people that control a country or an organization

temple a building where people pray to a god or gods

terrifying very frightening

Thanksgiving Day a national American holiday

therapist a specialist trained to help people by discussing their problems with them

tile a flat square of hard material, used on walls, floors, and roofs

tower a tall narrow building or part of a building

union joining two or more things together

vacations (*American English*) holidays

yoga a Hindu philosophy that teaches you how to control your body and mind; also, body and breathing exercises

ACTIVITIES

Before Reading

1 Read the introduction on the first page of the book, and the back cover. What do you know now about Elizabeth Gilbert? Choose T (True) or F (False) for each of these sentences.

1 Elizabeth Gilbert is a successful writer. T / F
2 She wants to have a baby. T / F
3 She divorces her husband. T / F
4 She travels around the world looking for a new relationship. T / F
5 She spends time in an Ashram in India. T / F

2 What do you think will happen to Elizabeth Gilbert on her travels? Choose Y (Yes) or N (No) for each of these ideas.

1 She will decide she wants to have a baby. Y / N
2 She will fall in love with someone. Y / N
3 She will go to live with the Balinese medicine man. Y / N
4 She will decide not to go back to New York. Y / N

3 In the introduction there is some advice for Elizabeth Gilbert from a Balinese medicine man. What do you think this means? Do you think it is good advice?

'You must have your feet strongly on the ground, but you must not look at the world through your head. You must look through your heart.'

ACTIVITIES

After Reading

1 Perhaps this is what some of the characters in the story are thinking. Which characters are they, and who or what are they thinking about? What is happening in the story at the moment?

Felipe / Giovanni / Ketut Liyer / Luca Spaghetti / Sofie / Wayan

1 'I am here in this beautiful house with all these wonderful people, and this amazing food . . . What a day! I couldn't ask for anything more!'

2 'It's perfect. It's close to town, and it has good *taksu*. She should definitely buy it.'

3 'I hope she knows what she is doing. What if she loses it? All those pictures, those mantras. What would my father say? My grandfather? My great-grandfather?'

4 'Oh my God, why is she crying like this? What am I going to say to her? We'll drive for a bit, and perhaps she'll calm down. Then we can talk.'

5 'I don't understand it! I can't believe it! Why have all these people done this for me? They don't even know me!'

6 'It is so good – so delicious! It really is the best in the world!'

2 There are 24 words (3 letters or longer) from the story in this word search. Find the words (they go from left to right, and from top to bottom), and draw lines through them.

W	A	T	C	S	E	A	R	C	H	P	H	T	M
H	E	C	R	Y	O	G	A	F	F	A	I	R	A
M	E	D	I	T	A	T	I	O	N	S	S	B	R
D	E	P	R	E	S	S	I	O	N	T	T	A	R
P	A	P	O	G	D	R	S	C	O	A	M	L	I
I	F	R	M	U	I	H	E	A	L	E	R	A	A
Z	L	A	A	R	V	E	I	T	A	L	Y	N	G
Z	I	Y	N	U	O	O	K	I	S	S	U	C	E
A	R	H	T	T	R	A	V	E	L	O	V	E	T
A	T	U	I	N	C	H	A	N	T	D	E	A	T
L	E	G	C	T	E	G	A	S	H	R	A	M	O

3 Now use 12 words from the word search to complete Liz's email to her sister.

Only a week left here in _____ now, but before I leave I've decided to _____ through Sicily. It's been an amazing few months, and I'm going to miss the _____ and _____, and all the wonderful people I've met here too! India will be very different. I wonder what life will be like in the _____, and if I will see my _____ there! I'm looking forward to doing some _____ and _____ and having all day to _____ and _____. I hope I won't _____ quite as much there – I need to lose some weight!

    Sending you a big _____!

      Liz

4 **Now write another email from Liz to her sister, this time from Bali. Try to use these six words from the word search.**

affair / balance / healer / love / romantic / search

5 **Look at the word search again, and write down all the letters without a line through them. Begin with the first line, and go across each line to the end. You should have 28 letters, which will make a sentence of 8 words.**

   1 What is the sentence, and who said it, to whom?
   2 What did the speaker want this person to do?
   3 Do you think it was good advice? Why?

6 **Complete this conversation between Wayan and Liz. Use as many words as you like.**

WAYAN: Bad news today, Liz. My rent is going up again.

LIZ: Will you be able to pay it?

WAYAN: _____

LIZ: What about Tutti?

WAYAN: _____

LIZ: Can you go and live with your family?

WAYAN: _____

LIZ: So what are you going to do?

WAYAN: _____

LIZ: Build your own house? That's exciting! So it's easy and cheap to buy land here, is it?

WAYAN: _____

LIZ: Oh dear!

7 **Here is what Felipe tells his friend about Wayan. Put the parts of sentences in the right order, and join them with these linking words to make a paragraph of four sentences.**

and / because / but / so

1 Then she began to play around with Liz, saying she needed more money, . . .

2 Liz asked her friends to give money to help Wayan buy a house, . . .

3 We think that really frightened Wayan, . . .

4 Wayan started to look for a house, . . .

5 _____ just four hours later she bought a piece of land!

6 _____ nothing seemed to be right for her.

7 _____ Liz said that her friends wanted to take the money back.

8 _____ after only a week she had almost $18,000.

8 **Which of these qualities are important when you decide to marry someone? Put them in order (1 for the most important). Explain why. Add any other ideas of your own.**

It is important to marry someone . . .

- who has a lot of money.
- that your parents like.
- who is handsome/pretty.
- who is interesting.
- who is older/younger than you.
- that you love.
- who loves you.
- who is clever.
- who is good.
- who is fun.

Which of these qualities do you think are important for Elizabeth Gilbert?

ABOUT THE AUTHOR

Elizabeth Gilbert was born in Connecticut, USA, in 1969, and grew up on the family farm. After studying at New York University, she traveled around the United States, working in bars, restaurants, and farms, listening to how people spoke, and finding ideas for stories. 'I made a vow to writing, very young,' she writes on her website. 'I built my entire life around writing. I didn't know how else to do this. I didn't know anyone who had ever become a writer. I had no clues. I just began.'

Gilbert's favorite writer is Charles Dickens, but as a child she loved the book *The Wizard of Oz*. 'I am a writer today,' she writes in a blog, 'because I learned to love reading as a child – and mostly on account of the Oz books.'

Her first book was *Pilgrims* (1997), a collection of short stories. This was followed by a novel, *Stern Men* (2000), and a biography, *The Last American Man* (2002). She is also a journalist, and both her books and her journalism have won prizes and awards. An article she wrote for GQ magazine about working in a New York bar resulted in the movie *Coyote Ugly*. Another novel is *The Signature of All Things* (2013).

However, she is best known for her 2006 memoir, *Eat, Pray, Love: One Woman's Search for Everything*, which became an international bestseller and has sold over 10 million copies. In 2010, it was made into a film, with Julia Roberts as Liz Gilbert. In the same year Gilbert published a follow-up memoir called *Committed: A Love Story*, which explores her feelings about marriage, and describes how she and Felipe, the Brazilian man from *Eat, Pray, Love*, finally got married. They now live in New Jersey, USA.

OXFORD BOOKWORMS LIBRARY

Classics • Crime & Mystery • Factfiles • Fantasy & Horror
Human Interest • Playscripts • Thriller & Adventure
True Stories • World Stories

The OXFORD BOOKWORMS LIBRARY provides enjoyable reading in English, with a wide range of classic and modern fiction, non-fiction, and plays. It includes original and adapted texts in seven carefully graded language stages, which take learners from beginner to advanced level. An overview is given on the next pages.

All Stage 1 titles are available as audio recordings, as well as over eighty other titles from Starter to Stage 6. All Starters and many titles at Stages 1 to 4 are specially recommended for younger learners. Every Bookworm is illustrated, and Starters and Factfiles have full-colour illustrations.

The OXFORD BOOKWORMS LIBRARY also offers extensive support. Each book contains an introduction to the story, notes about the author, a glossary, and activities. Additional resources include tests and worksheets, and answers for these and for the activities in the books. There is advice on running a class library, using audio recordings, and the many ways of using Oxford Bookworms in reading programmes. Resource materials are available on the website <www.oup.com/elt/gradedreaders>.

The *Oxford Bookworms Collection* is a series for advanced learners. It consists of volumes of short stories by well-known authors, both classic and modern. Texts are not abridged or adapted in any way, but carefully selected to be accessible to the advanced student.

You can find details and a full list of titles in the *Oxford Bookworms Library Catalogue* and *Oxford English Language Teaching Catalogues*, and on the website <www.oup.com/elt/gradedreaders>.

THE OXFORD BOOKWORMS LIBRARY
GRADING AND SAMPLE EXTRACTS

STARTER • 250 HEADWORDS

present simple – present continuous – imperative –
can/cannot, must – going to (future) – simple gerunds ...

Her phone is ringing – but where is it?

Sally gets out of bed and looks in her bag. No phone. She looks under the bed. No phone. Then she looks behind the door. There is her phone. Sally picks up her phone and answers it. *Sally's Phone*

STAGE 1 • 400 HEADWORDS

... past simple – coordination with *and*, *but*, *or* –
subordination with *before*, *after*, *when*, *because*, *so* ...

I knew him in Persia. He was a famous builder and I worked with him there. For a time I was his friend, but not for long. When he came to Paris, I came after him – I wanted to watch him. He was a very clever, very dangerous man. *The Phantom of the Opera*

STAGE 2 • 700 HEADWORDS

... present perfect – *will* (future) – (*don't*) have to, must not, could –
comparison of adjectives – simple *if* clauses – past continuous –
tag questions – *ask/tell* + infinitive ...

While I was writing these words in my diary, I decided what to do. I must try to escape. I shall try to get down the wall outside. The window is high above the ground, but I have to try. I shall take some of the gold with me – if I escape, perhaps it will be helpful later. *Dracula*

STAGE 3 • 1000 HEADWORDS

... should, may – present perfect continuous – *used to* – past perfect –
causative – relative clauses – indirect statements ...

Of course, it was most important that no one should see
Colin, Mary, or Dickon entering the secret garden. So Colin
gave orders to the gardeners that they must all keep away
from that part of the garden in future. *The Secret Garden*

STAGE 4 • 1400 HEADWORDS

... past perfect continuous – passive (simple forms) –
would conditional clauses – indirect questions –
relatives with *where/when* – gerunds after prepositions/phrases ...

I was glad. Now Hyde could not show his face to the world
again. If he did, every honest man in London would be
proud to report him to the police. *Dr Jekyll and Mr Hyde*

STAGE 5 • 1800 HEADWORDS

... future continuous – future perfect –
passive (modals, continuous forms) –
would have conditional clauses – modals + perfect infinitive ...

If he had spoken Estella's name, I would have hit him. I was
so angry with him, and so depressed about my future, that I
could not eat the breakfast. Instead I went straight to the old
house. *Great Expectations*

STAGE 6 • 2500 HEADWORDS

... passive (infinitives, gerunds) – advanced modal meanings –
clauses of concession, condition

When I stepped up to the piano, I was confident. It was as if
I knew that the prodigy side of me really did exist. And when I
started to play, I was so caught up in how lovely I looked that I
didn't worry how I would sound. *The Joy Luck Club*

Desert, Mountain, Sea

SUE LEATHER

Three different parts of the world, but all of them dangerous, lonely places. Three different women, but all of them determined to go – and to come back alive!

Robyn Davidson walked nearly 3,000 kilometres across the Australian desert – with a dog and four camels.

Arlene Blum led a team of ten women to the top of Annapurna – one of the highest mountains in the world. Only eight came down again.

Naomi James sailed around the world alone, on a journey lasting more than 250 days.

Three real adventures – three really adventurous women.

A Dubious Legacy

MARY WESLEY

Retold by Rosalie Kerr

In 1944 Henry Tillotson brings his new wife, Margaret, home to his farmhouse in the English countryside. Margaret is a strange, unpleasant woman, determined, it seems, to make Henry's life miserable. 'Poor Henry!' say his friends, as they visit at weekends and holidays. 'What an awful life he has!' But Henry is not at all the sad and disappointed man we might expect him to be. He manages to enjoy life, and indeed, has quite a lot of fun, one way and another . . .

Mary Wesley's story takes a sharp but light-hearted look at love, sex, and marriage – and the things people will do to get what they want.